BARCELONA 2014

THE CITY AT A GLANCE

Torre Agbar
Rising from Plaça de les Glòries Catalanes,
Jean Nouvel's multicoloured tower is home to
the offices of the Agbar water c
at its most spectacular when vi
See p012

GW00537493

Hotel Arts
Built for the 1992 Olympic Gam
city's first modern luxury hotel i
grande dame of Barcelona's seaf
Pompidou-style steel exoskeleto
the traditional comforts that lie v
Carrer de la Marina 19-21, T 93 221 1000

Sagrada Família
Work started in 1882 on Gaudí's unfinished
masterpiece, an enduring symbol of the
Catalan capital. The gothic structure, which
will stand at 170m when finally complete,
is constructed from up to 30 types of stone.
Carrer de Mallorca 401, T 93 513 2060

W hotel
Known locally as *la vela* (the sail) for its
distinctive shape, the W is visible from all over
the city and has prompted the regeneration
of a previously unkempt section of beachfront.
See p013

Santa Maria del Pi
Medieval architect Bartomeu Mas designed
this Barri Gòtic church's 54m-high octagonal
belfry, which was completed in 1461.
Plaça del Pi 7, T 93 318 4743

Castell de Montjuïc
Once a loathed fortress used as a base to
oppress the city's own residents, this castle
is now a leisure zone, hosting festivals,
outdoor film-screenings and concerts.
Carretera de Montjuïc 66, T 93 329 8653

INTRODUCTION
THE CHANGING FACE OF THE URBAN SCENE

It is a rare thing for a city to reinvent itself so thoroughly, but Barcelona's change of fortune after the 1992 Olympic Games was the envy of the world. What was once considered a scruffy port town was suddenly held up as a model of urban planning and glacial cool, and throughout the 1990s there was nowhere more fashionable to spend a long weekend. Then, inevitably, came the backlash, when the city arguably became the victim of its own success. As the conventioneers and cruise ships began to throng into town, Barna's distinctive scene became, well, a tad bridge-and-tunnel. Smarter travellers shifted south to Valencia or to the Balearics, but more recently they've been coming back, lured by the achingly hip hotels, happening bars and radical cuisine.

For architecture junkies, the city's pickings are rich. Gaudí's modernista legacy is enriched by the work of a string of leading contemporary architects (Santiago Calatrava, EMBT and Foster + Partners among them). Slated to open in 2014 is MBM's Disseny Hub (see po68), which will showcase design and decorative arts collections under one roof, and should complement the number of excellent museums already resident in Barcelona, including the CaixaForum art space (see po32), CCCB (see po35) and the great art palace MNAC (Palau Nacional, Parc de Montjuïc, T 93 622 0360). Spirited, cool and style-savvy, Barcelona is far more than the Catalan capital. Come to see for yourself.

ESSENTIAL INFO

FACTS, FIGURES AND USEFUL ADDRESSES

TOURIST OFFICE
Plaça de Catalunya 17
T 93 285 3834
www.barcelonaturisme.com

TRANSPORT
Airport transfer to city centre
The Aerobús departs regularly between
6am and 1am. The journey takes 35 minutes
www.aerobusbcn.com
Car hire
Avis
T 90 211 0275
Metro
Trains run from 5am to 12am, Sunday to
Thursday; 5am to 2am on Fridays; and
for 24 hours on Saturdays
www.tmb.net
Taxis
Ràdio Taxi 033
T 93 303 3033
Tourist card
A three-day Barcelona Card (€47) grants
free travel and entry to many attractions

EMERGENCY SERVICES
Emergencies
T 112
Late-night pharmacy
Farmàcia Álvarez
Passeig de Gràcia 26
T 93 302 1124

CONSULATES
British Consulate-General
13th floor, Avinguda Diagonal 477
T 90 210 9356
www.gov.uk/government/world/spain
US Consulate-General
Passeig Reina Elisenda de Montcada 23
T 93 280 2227
barcelona.usconsulate.gov

POSTAL SERVICES
Post office
Correo Central
Plaça Antonio López
T 93 486 8302
Shipping
UPS (Mail Boxes Etc)
Carrer de València 214
T 93 454 6983

BOOKS
Barcelona
by Robert Hughes (Vintage)
Homage To Catalonia
by George Orwell (Penguin Classics)

WEBSITES
Architecture
www.coac.net
www.gaudi2002.bcn.es
www.rutadelmodernisme.com
Newspapers
www.elpais.com
www.lavanguardia.com

EVENTS
Barcelona Design Week
www.barcelonadesignweek.com
LOOP Fair
www.loop-barcelona.com

COST OF LIVING
Taxi from El Prat Airport to city centre
€25
Cappuccino
€1.45
Packet of cigarettes
€4.70
Daily newspaper
€1.30
Bottle of champagne
€60

BARCELONA
Population
1.62 million
Currency
Euro
Telephone codes
Spain: 34
Barcelona: 93
Local time
GMT +1
Flight time
London: 2 hours

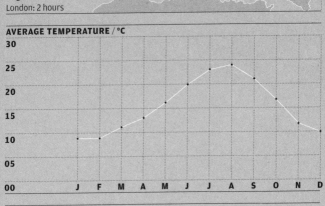

AVERAGE TEMPERATURE / °C

30
25
20
15
10
05
00

J F M A M J J A S O N D

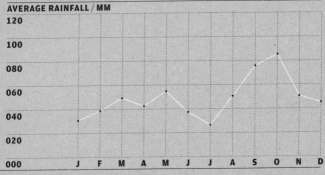

AVERAGE RAINFALL / MM

120
100
080
060
040
020
000

J F M A M J J A S O N D

NEIGHBOURHOODS

THE AREAS YOU NEED TO KNOW AND WHY

To help you navigate the city, we've chosen the most interesting districts (see below and the map inside the back cover) and colour-coded our featured venues, according to their location; those venues that are outside these areas are not coloured.

EIXAMPLE

This sizeable district (which translates as 'extension') is where most of the city's modernista gems are located, including the Sagrada Família (see p009), Casa Milà (see p014) and Casa Batlló (see p034). The elegant Passeig de Gràcia, a power-shopping strip, cuts through the area.

BARRI GÒTIC

The most atmospheric part of Barna, the Gothic Quarter dates back to Roman times. Its winding medieval streets are lorded over by the city's main cathedral and are dotted with artisans' shops, particularly around Plaça del Pi and Plaça de Sant Just. Eat and drink at the multi-faceted Ocaña (see p046) on Plaça Reial.

BARCELONETA

Complete with manmade beaches created for the Olympics, this upscale pleasure ground is packed with restaurants and bars overlooking the marina. Gentrification is heading down south into Platja de Sant Sebastià with the launch of venues such as the breezy Pez Vela (see p061).

GRÀCIA

It is whispered that Gràcia is becoming the city's hippest 'hood. Boho and pretty, and peppered with one-off boutiques, it has an independent spirit and a friendly, villagey ambience. Nearby, check out Casa Vicens (Carrer de les Carolines 24), a lesser-known Gaudí-designed building.

POBLE SEC

Residential and laidback, Poble Sec is a pleasant place to wander after visiting the parks and museums of Montjuïc, the city's expansive hilltop parkland. There is a string of cute cafés along Carrer de Blai, and, close by, a tapas institution in the form of Quimet & Quimet (see p056).

POBLENOU

Upwardly mobile, loft-dwelling creatives are transforming this area, carving studios out of disused warehouses and factories. To the north-east, the residential and tourist development Diagonal Mar (see p064) is the site of bold skyscrapers, but we'd favour checking into the ME hotel (see p016) in the nascent business district.

RAVAL

Visit Raval to witness Barcelona's most aggressive gentrification over the past few years. Upper Raval has swapped its edgy vibe for an arty one, and it's now home to the cultural centres MACBA (see p032) and CCCB (see p035), boutiques, bars and restaurants, such as Dos Palillos (see p052).

SANT PERE/BORN

Museu Picasso (see p032) and the Gothic Santa Maria del Mar church are Born's crowd-pleasers, and the shopping here is the best in town, especially for fashion and design. Sant Pere is an up-and-coming zone; standing proud as its centrepiece is the Mercat de Santa Caterina (see p009).

LANDMARKS
THE SHAPE OF THE CITY SKYLINE

The economic downturn has hit Barcelona hard, and several key architectural projects are on hold or are proceeding at a snail's pace. However, their sheer ambition still dazzles, and ideas that came to fruition just before the recession have, for the most part, been rapturously received. The site of the 2004 Universal Forum of Cultures, including Herzog & de Meuron's triangular Edifici Fòrum (see p064) housing Museu Blau, has become a familiar facet of local life, and Jean Nouvel's flashy Torre Agbar (see p012) anchors the dotcom zone at the eastern end of Avinguda Diagonal.

Architects have long since turned their attention to the city's western flank. David Chipperfield's massive Ciutat de la Justícia (overleaf) was completed in 2009, and Richard Rogers converted the former bullring, Las Arenas (Gran Via de les Corts Catalanes 373-385, T 93 289 0244), into a gleaming shopping centre in 2011. Meanwhile, the gentrification of the old city, which hit its high note with the Mercat de Santa Caterina (Avinguda de Francesc Cambó 16), seemingly knows no end. Amid this upheaval it is comforting to cling to the familiar. Casa Milà (see p014), Gaudí's first purpose-built apartment block, begun in 1906 – the year he finished Casa Batlló (see p034) – offers a selection of his unique design riffs for when the hawkers and handycams at the Sagrada Família (Carrer de Mallorca 401, T 93 513 2060) become too much. *For full addresses, see Resources.*

Ciutat de la Justícia

Barcelonins who appreciate good architecture – as well as all those unfortunates who face the prospect of navigating Spain's highly complicated legal system – are jumping for joy that David Chipperfield's Ciutat de la Justícia, or 'City of Justice', didn't get canned (as so many other large-scale projects did) when the fallout from the global economic meltdown hit the country.

Situated at Barcelona's westernmost point of entry, the complex comprises nine buildings, and accommodates law courts and public offices relating to the bar and forensic practices, grouping together what was previously a set of 17 different edifices scattered across the city. Public plazas and a connecting concourse add ease of communication. *Gran Via de les Corts Catalanes*

Torre Agbar

Jean Nouvel's 142m structure became a defining feature of the Barcelona skyline after its completion in 2005. Unless you are a prospective tenant of the offices inside, it's unlikely you'll gain access to the steel-and-glass interior, but it's easy to appreciate the 4,500-windowed tower from Plaça de les Glòries Catalanes. Agbar is the local water company, something that Nouvel seldom tired of referencing in the design. The sensuous exterior of the building resembles a stream of bubbling water; its surface appears to ripple under a liquid film. The top floors are clad in clear glass, below which metal panels descend in tones of white and blue, before meeting the violent orange, fuchsia and red panels that rise from the base.

Plaça de les Glòries Catalanes,
www.torreagbar.com

W hotel

Barcelona architect Ricardo Bofill is one of Spain's most prolific. Yet despite his global status, his hometown projects are surprisingly few. Two major works in 2009 addressed that: the elegant airport terminal and the W. The soaring, sail-shaped hotel sits at the point where the city's beach gives way to the sea, and together with Hotel Arts (see p016), it punctuates this stretch of sand like a bookend. But it is the W that is most arresting: at 90m high, it is the first distinguishable form that many visitors see, whether they arrive by air or by sea. The project, which includes a boardwalk, a plaza and a pending medical research centre, all by Bofill, has opened up a little pocket of Barcelona's precious shoreline.
Plaça de la Rosa dels Vents 1,
T 93 295 2800, www.w-barcelona.com

Casa Milà

This iconic 1912 residential building, with its wave-like facade, was Gaudí's last civil project before he secluded himself at the site of the Sagrada Família (see p009). Take a tour of the most important areas: a flat fitted out in the modernista decor of Gaudí's era, the roof, an exhibition space, and the Espai Gaudí – a showcase of the architect's creations – in the attic.
Carrer Provença 261-265, T 90 220 2138

HOTELS

WHERE TO STAY AND WHICH ROOMS TO BOOK

This is a city brimming with great hotels, and the high level of competition keeps the best on their toes. The number of four- and five-star openings in the past few years has pushed Barcelona's early design-led properties, such as Claris Hotel (Carrer de Pau Claris 150, T 93 487 6262) and Hotel Arts (Carrer de la Marina 19-21, T 93 221 1000), to fight harder to draw a savvy clientele. Although the former still has a loyal following, the latter invested in top-rate restaurants, like Enoteca (T 93 483 8108), which has two Michelin stars. Omm (see p028) joined in with the cool Roca Moo, and the Mandarin Oriental (see p022) unveiled Moments (T 93 151 8781).

Of the more recent arrivals, ME (Carrer de Pere IV 272, T 93 367 2050) occupies a sparkling Poblenou skyscraper designed by Dominique Perrault. In south-eastern Eixample, often referred to as Gayxample, is the luxury, gay-friendly Axel Hotel (Carrer d'Aribau 33, T 93 323 9393), whereas down in Barcelona's most (in)famous area, the reworked colonial Hotel 1898 (La Rambla 109, T 93 552 9552) is set in the former premises of the Philippines Tobacco Company. Period splendour can be found at the Bagués Hotel (see p020) and at the modernista Hotel España (Carrer de Sant Pau 9-11, T 93 550 0000). At the other end of the spectrum is The Mirror (Carrer de Còrsega 255, T 93 202 8686), which opened in 2011 and has a pristine, almost clinical interior.

For full addresses and room rates, see Resources.

Alma

Opened in 2011 after a refurbishment by Catalan firms Habitan Arquitectos and CoriumCasa, Alma combines the original features of its early 20th-century setting in Eixample with contemporary touches. Cornicing and parquet flooring are paired with Casamilano chairs, Contardi lamps and subtly lit charcoal-hued corridors that pave the way to the 72 spacious, high-ceilinged rooms. The street-facing accommodations lean towards the classic, while those that overlook the garden have more modern interiors, boasting floor-to-ceiling windows and muslin shades. Sofas by Tacchini are scattered throughout the lobby (above) to encourage lounging, but the quiet terrace is the best spot to enjoy a cocktail, oblivious to the traffic outside. *Carrer de Mallorca 271, T 93 216 4490, www.almabarcelona.com*

Mercer Hotel

A world removed from the tourist bustle a short walk away, the Mercer, a sympathetic reimagining of a building that has parts dating back to the Roman era, exudes a cool, high-ceilinged calm. Fittingly for a hotel located in Barcelona's Gothic Quarter, the design – overseen by architect Rafael Moneo – incorporates an excess of original features. These include wooden coffered ceilings, bare stone walls, gothic windows, medieval columns and a Roman-period watchtower, which was once part of the walls circling the city. Neutral-toned rooms like the Gran Deluxe (above), overlook a central orange-tree-filled patio, addressing the lack of natural light that plagues Barri Gòtic buildings. For direct sun, head up to the decked rooftop terrace and pool.
Carrer dels Lledó 7, T 93 310 2387, www.mercerbarcelona.com

Bagués Hotel
This bijou residence, which has only
31 rooms, pays homage to its former
occupants, the jewellers Bagués, at
almost every turn. Rich colours, fluid
furnishings and fittings abound in rooms
such as the Jewel Suite (pictured). There
is even a museum displaying enamel
pieces by master jeweller Masriera.
La Rambla 105, T 93 343 5000,
www.derbyhotels.com

Mandarin Oriental

Launched in 2009, the Mandarin Oriental stands out for its sophisticated design aesthetic. The entire interior is the work of Patricia Urquiola, the Milan-based Spanish designer. Handwoven carpets, modernist decor and a hanging garden are just some of the hotel's highlights; Urquiola drew inspiration from the Mandarin Group's Asian heritage, as well as the elegance of the 1950s building, originally a bank's headquarters. The suites deserve their high price tags; we like the Barcelona (above). But you may spend more time in public areas like the snug Banker's Bar (order the Ginger Martini), Catalan restaurant Moments (see p016), headed by the son of star chef Carme Ruscalleda, or Blanc, a restaurant-cum-lounge. *Passeig de Gràcia 38-40, T 93 151 8888, www.mandarinoriental.com/barcelona*

Hotel DO: Plaça Reial

'Boutique hotel' is a much abused term these days, but the DO embodies the concept; a small, stylish, family-owned property comprising just 18 rooms (Junior Suite, above). Architect Oriol Bohigas and interior designer Lázaro Rosa-Violán are the men responsible for this sophisticated affair, utilising mismatched pieces of furniture, hardwood floors, reclaimed beams and colourful rugs — even the wooden stationery trays are covetable. Unusually, breakfast, the (non-alcoholic) contents of the minibar, wi-fi and an hour in the sauna and steam room are included in the rate. Located just off La Rambla, the hotel has a roof terrace with a plunge pool and fine views of the handsome, arcaded Plaça Reial and the city beyond.
Plaça Reial 1, T 93 481 3666,
www.hoteldoreial.com

Ohla Hotel

Situated in a neoclassical former police headquarters in Barri Gòtic, the Ohla is easily recognisable due to Barcelona artist Frederic Amat's quirky eyeball sculptures studded over the hotel's facade. Equally diverting is the main interior staircase (opposite). The 74 rooms, including the Junior Suite (above), are comfortable, spacious and simple, and the rooftop terrace has a glass-sided swimming pool and great views. But it's the service that really stands out: guests can personalise sheets, pillows and even the scent of the bedlinen; laptops, iPods and breakfast-to-go backpacks are also available. Top chef Xavier Franco chose the hotel as home for Saüc (T 93 321 0189), his Michelin-starred restaurant, which serves Catalan cuisine. *Via Laietana 49, T 93 341 5050, www.ohlahotel.com*

El Palauet
Truly noble accommodation can be found
in this modernist mansion transformed
into six sumptuous self-catering suites.
Dating from 1906, the building was
designed by a contemporary of Gaudí's,
Pere Falqués, whose most famous work
is the iron streetlighting that lines Passeig
de Gràcia. El Palauet exposes all the
excesses of the epoch, with elaborately
carved woodwork, moulded ceilings
and delicate leadlight at every turn. The
proprietors have modernised the edifice
admirably, installing high-tech lighting,
bespoke Corian bathrooms and a creamy
decor that features pieces from Starck,
Jacobsen and Eames, among other key
20th-century designers. The best rooms
are rear-facing, like the Principal Tibidabo
Suite (left), which has a pretty, stained-
glass-enclosed *glorieta* (sun room).
Passeig de Gràcia 113, T 93 218 0050,
www.epliving barcelona.com

Hotel Omm

Grupo Tragaluz's first hotel venture, in 2004, went down a storm with the city's beautiful people, who still grace Omm's 1950s-style lounge bar (above), furnished with Arne Jacobsen 'Egg' chairs and 'Visor' lamps. Heading up to one of the 91 rooms is like walking a futuristic catwalk, thanks to the strip lighting. Many Omm King and Superior rooms have balconies looking over the inner courtyard; those facing the street have windows tucked behind the peeled-back panels of the hotel's facade. The rooftop pool – from where you can spy Casa Milà (see p014) – and Spaciomm spa (T 93 445 4949) cater to the preened and terminally hip, as do the in-house Roca Moo restaurant, Roca Bar, opened in 2013, and basement club Ommsession.
Carrer Rosselló 265, T 93 445 4000, www.hotelomm.es

Barceló Raval

Hotel Barceló Raval sits on the Rambla del Raval, the busy gathering point of the city's most populous (and many would say edgiest) neighbourhood. Given its location, this hotel is not for everyone. But if you want to savour the urban delights of Barcelona's infamous old city you'll love the rooftop terrace that affords fascinating 360-degree views. Downstairs, the funky *Twin Peaks*-inspired lobby (a work of local interiorista Jordi Galí) features fuchsia pink, lime-green and black decor, flock wallpaper and oversized faux-Regency furniture. Thankfully, the hotel's spacious rooms are more pared down, with modular, acrylic-white fittings and vistas filtered through the structure's metal-mesh facade. We recommend the Junior Suite (above). *Rambla del Raval 17-21, T 93 320 1490, www.barcelo.com*

W

The location and size of Barcelona's W (see p013) should tell you it is not for shrinking violets. Wearing its party credentials loud and proud, the W burst on to the scene in 2009 with the longest calendar of Moët-flowing 'opening parties' in living memory and has barely drawn breath since. This hip little resort promotes such a hedonistic Ibiza vibe that guests need never leave. After a morning at the in-house Bliss Spa (T 93 295 2658), and an afternoon on the wet deck, dine at Bravo (T 93 295 2636) and then head on up to the top-storey Eclipse (T 93 295 2800) dance bar. Although rooms may lack the pizzazz of common areas such as the lobby, they have great sea views. We particularly like the Cool Corner Suite (above).
Plaça de la Rosa dels Vents 1,
T 93 295 2800, www.w-barcelona.com

Suites Avenue

An arresting slit-steel facade by Japanese architect Toyo Ito announces that Suites Avenue stands apart from the plethora of holiday apartments proliferating in Barcelona's old town. For starters, it is run by the Spanish Derby Hotels Group, pioneers in luxury accommodation. And its location on upmarket Passeig de Gràcia means it rubs shoulders with modernist masterworks such as Casa Milà (see p014) and Casa Batlló (see p034), and the Pedrera Penthouse offers fantastic views. Services include a 24/7 concierge, two outdoor pools and a gym. Suites Avenue is also one of the few pet-friendly luxe options in Barcelona. If you wish to self-cater, the kitchens are so well equipped that they even have a wine fridge.
Passeig de Gràcia 83, T 93 487 4159, www.derbyhotels.com

24 HOURS

SEE THE BEST OF THE CITY IN JUST ONE DAY

Barcelona has such a captivating range of architecture and world-class museums that, on a first foray, even the most organised visitor will only be able to scratch the surface. It would be impertinent not to pay some respect to Gaudí's genius, and, despite the fact that it's still unfinished, the Sagrada Família (see p009) remains *the* most arresting structure in Barcelona. If you're more interested in the city's heritage, skip MACBA (Plaça dels Àngels 1, T 93 412 0810) and CCCB (see p035) and head to Palau de la Música (Carrer Palau de la Música 4-6, T 90 244 2882), or Museu Picasso (Carrer de Montcada 15-23, T 93 256 3000), which charts the evolution of the painter's oeuvre. In Poblenou, the Disseny Hub (see p068), when it fully opens in spring 2014, will bring together the city's decorative arts museums under one roof.

Head towards Montjuïc to visit Fundació Joan Miró (see p036) and the Mies van der Rohe Pavilion (see p070), a reassembly of his seminal modernist building for the 1929 World's Fair. Nearby, CaixaForum (Avinguda de Francesc Ferrer i Guàrdia 6-8, T 93 476 8600) puts on touring exhibitions that are always worth a look. Afterwards, chill out in front of the Font Màgica de Montjuïc (Plaça de Carles Buïgas), a night-time extravaganza of water jets that dance to an eclectic soundtrack, from Abba to Tchaikovsky (times are listed on www.barcelonaturisme.com).

For full addresses, see Resources.

10.00 Cornelia and Co

This deli-style café, which opened in 2010, was inspired in part by New York's Dean & DeLuca, and has canteen-style decor by Barcelona-based architects GCA and branding by graphics studio The Own. It makes an interesting change from the countless bars in the city that only offer a coffee and croissant in the morning: try a *batido* (smoothie) or freshly squeezed juice, and choose from a selection of bread and muffins. You could also put together a picnic-style lunch, with sandwiches and gourmet baked goods, salads, pasta and rice, farmhouse cheeses and even fresh oysters available to eat in or take away. A range of wines, condiments and other epicurean edibles are displayed along the walls. Open from noon on weekdays.
Carrer de València 225, T 93 272 3956, www.corneliaandco.com

11.30 Casa Batlló

For the full Gaudí experience, head to the elegant Passeig de Gràcia and 'Manzana de la Discòrdia' (Block of Discord), home to three key modernista buildings. Casa Amatller (No 41) and Casa Lleò Morera (see p085) complete the trio, but the centrepiece is Casa Batlló, one of Gaudí's most distinctive structures – a renovation of an existing building finished in 1906. The *trencadis* (broken tile) mosaic that blankets the facade is mesmerising, but then so is the surreal, undulating interior. Among the highlights are the drawing room and its stained-glass windows that have sinuous frames; the spine-like stairwell; and the shimmering, tile-clad roof, said to represent the dragon slain by Catalonia's patron saint, Jordi.
Passeig de Gràcia 43, T 93 216 0306, www.casabatllo.es

15.00 CCCB

Spanish architects Albert Viaplana and Helio Piñón renovated the Casa de la Caritat almshouse in 1994, adding a glass facade to create what has now become a cultural hub for art and music. As well as curating a programme of some of the most absorbing exhibitions in town, CCCB (Centre de Cultura Contemporània de Barcelona) hosts a cross-section of multidisciplinary festivals, debates, lectures, concerts and courses. Each August it presents 'Gandules', a series of outdoor cinema screenings, showing often overlooked international films. Next door is contemporary art museum MACBA (see p032), designed by Richard Meier, which displays modern Catalan and international artwork.
Carrer de Montalegre 5, T 93 306 4100, www.cccb.org

17.30 Fundació Joan Miró

Surrealist artist Joan Miró had his work mocked for many years in his home town; it was only when he moved to Paris that he found the recognition he deserved. Finally, in 1975 (when Miró was 82), he was honoured with this museum, housed in a rationalist building by architect Josep Lluís Sert. Its low-slung appearance belies the airy spaces within – ideal for Miró's vast canvases and sculptures (*The Caress of a Bird*, above left) – and its white walls and roof terraces dazzle in the sun. Fundació Miró hosts exhibitions of modern artists too; Jackson Pollock, Mona Hatoum and Pipilotti Rist have featured in recent years, and Alexander Calder's *Mercury Fountain* has a permanent home here. Closed Mondays, and Sundays from 2.30pm. *Parc de Montjuïc, T 93 443 9470, www.fundaciomiro-bcn.org*

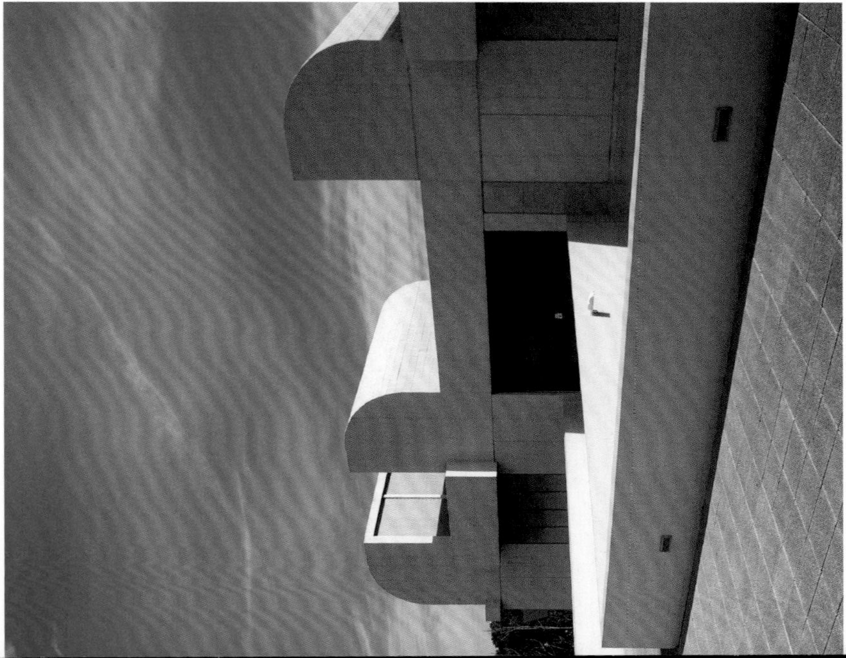

21.00 Tickets/41º Experience

In 2011, super-chef Ferran Adrià and his brother Albert (once pastry chef at the now-closed elBulli restaurant) breathed some culinary life into an unfashionable part of town with the opening of Tickets and 41º Experience. Situated next door to each other, the two venues are connected via a passageway. Tickets (above) offers tapas in a playful space, serving traditional morsels alongside Adrià's signature molecular cuisine, such as liquid ravioli with payoyo cheese. Bar 41º (opposite) is decked out with leather banquettes and bull's head sculptures, and presents an innovative menu before 11.30pm, made up of 41 different dishes. After this, the bar focuses on the fine art of cocktail making. Book well ahead, online.
Avinguda del Paral·lel 164,
www.ca.bcn50.org

URBAN LIFE
CAFÉS, RESTAURANTS, BARS AND NIGHTCLUBS

The birth of Barcelona's distinct style of Catalan cuisine is thanks largely to the success of the culinary mecca elBulli on the Costa Brava, many times voted the world's best restaurant before it was closed by chef Ferran Adrià in 2011. In its place, Adrià founded a gastronomic research centre, and in 2011 opened up a tapas bar, Tickets/41° Experience (see p038). Many in the city have tried to replicate Adrià's formula, with varying degrees of success. One of the best attempts is Comerç 24 (Carrer del Comerç 24, T 93 319 2102), run by elBulli alumnus Carles Abellan. Conservative palates should stick to trad venues such as 7 Portes (Passeig d'Isabel II 14, T 93 319 3033) and Can Ravell (Carrer d'Aragó 313, T 93 457 5114).

Art junkies can combine a visit to Museu Picasso (see p032) with a meal at Els 4 Gats (Carrer Montsió 3, T 93 302 4140), where the artist picked up his first commission, to design the menu. More than a century later, it's still in use, and some of his early sketches adorn the walls. Gaudí fans should ensure they reserve a table at the Casa Calvet (Carrer de Casp 48, T 93 412 4012) in the building of the same name, which was designed by the architect. For a post-dinner drink, head to Xixbar (Carrer de Rocafort 19, T 93 423 4314), which has spearheaded the city craze for *gintónics* by way of 130 brands of gin, or Cocktail Bar Juanra Falces (Carrer del Rec 24, T 93 310 1027), which closes only when the last person leaves. *For full addresses, see Resources.*

Chez Cocó

This restaurant, opened in 2012, makes a bold statement of intent at the entrance, where diners walk right by the long, open kitchen, festooned with copper pans and backed by a wall of rotisserie spits on which every conceivable fowl can be seen slowly rotating. The dining room is equally thrilling, all soaring ceilings, dark oak panelling, chandeliers, mosaic flooring, etched mirrors and a line of cobalt blue upholstered banquettes. The menu centres on chicken, along with guinea fowl, duck and the much maligned turkey, but the simplest and best dish is the roast poussin, served with a skillet of hand-cut chips. After dinner, patrons drift to the terrace bar, which is illuminated by large bulbs and lanterns, for a speciality G & T. *Avinguda Diagonal 465, T 93 444 9822, www.chezcoco.es*

MAT Bar

In the heart of Eixample's gay district, MAT Bar attracts a mixed but stylish clientele, drawn to its quirky decor, creative snacks and cocktails, and eclectic soundtrack (no handbag house here). Like most Eixample bars, it is a long and narrow space, cleverly broken up in the middle by an open kitchen kiosk. Wood-panelled walls are decorated with vintage sports equipment picked up on the Australian owners' travels, including table-tennis bats, lacrosse sticks, skipping ropes and wooden hula hoops. As well as cocktails, local artisanal beers and freshly ground coffee are served, and there are tasty platters of cheese and charcuterie as well as a small selection of pizzettas, which are topped with delicacies from the Middle East and the Med. Closed Mondays.
Carrer de Consell de Cent 245,
T 93 453 7722, www.matbar.es

Velódromo

This Barcelona institution reopened in 2009 as Velódromo, having been a much-loved meeting-point and *casino* (as in social club, not gambling den) from 1933 to 2000. Housed in one of the city's few true art deco buildings, it's a gem of a bar/restaurant, meticulously restored to recall the grandeur of the early 20th century. Pistachio-painted columns and matching banquettes, marble-tiled floors and an ornately carved and polished wood ceiling create an attractive backdrop to food overseen by Michelin-starred chef Jordi Vilà. Far removed from the well-trodden tourist trails of the city's downtown, and open from 6am to 3am, it's no surprise that locals have reclaimed it as their own, stopping by for early morning breakfasts or post-bar late-night snacks.

Carrer de Muntaner 213, T 93 430 6022

Dry Martini

Numerous *coctelerías* (cocktail bars) dot the grid of Eixample, but Dry Martini has remained the leader of the pack for more than three decades since opening in 1978. Although it's located on the ground floor of a 1970s apartment block, the decor is pure speakeasy: leather sofas form comfy conversation pits and liveried mixologists are ready and waiting with shakers in hand behind the mahogany bar. It's a hangout of Barcelona's intelligentsia, who make a beeline here at about 8.30pm for a *cubata* (mixed drink). After dinner, the scene gets a bit livelier, with drinkers of all stripes piling in from the nearby restaurants.
Carrer d'Aribau 162-166, T 93 217 5072, www.drymartinibcn.com

Ocaña
Plaça Reial, ignored by locals for years, is finally shaking off its tourist-trap image, partly thanks to the 2012 opening of Ocaña, which takes up most of its eastern flank. As well as a restaurant (pictured), this ambitious venture also features a café, a club and a cocktail bar, each with a different style, all linked by atriums and a terrace under the square's arcades.
Plaça Reial 13-15. T 93 676 4814

Cinc Sentits
Chef Jordi Artal and maître d' Amèlia Artal are the charming brother-and-sister team who run this elegant restaurant, which serves modern Catalan cuisine. The dining room was renovated in 2011 and now feels more intimate, with an undulating row of copper chains hanging from the ceiling and textured wood panelling on the once-white walls. The excellent tasting menus are available in either five-course form, or seven or 10 courses accompanied by wine pairings. If you order the 10 courses, savour the foie gras with vinegar-glazed leeks, and warm chocolate mousse with olive-oil ice cream. The Iberian suckling pig served with seasonal embellishments is one of the restaurant's signature dishes. Cinc Sentits has a global reputation, so it's advisable to book well in advance.
Carrer d'Aribau 58, T 93 323 9490, www.cincsentits.com

Boca Grande

Another project from interior designer Lázaro Rosa-Violán – also behind Hotel DO (see p023), Chez Cocó (see p041) and Big Fish (see p054) – Boca Grande bears all the hallmarks of his opulent yet cosy eclecticism. Seating in the wood-panelled restaurant (above) is plushly upholstered, and every surface is strewn with antiques, sketches or photographs. Most spectacular is the downstairs bathroom, dotted with vintage mirrors and banquettes, and thumping to a DJ mix. The seafood-heavy menu includes dishes such as scallops with Iberian ham, and ceviche. There's also an oyster bar and cocktail room, and upstairs is Boca Chica (opposite), a lavish bar with a colonial air. On the floor above that, The Apartment is a cosy lounge with a terrace. *Passatge de la Concepció 12, T 93 467 5149, www.bocagrande.cat*

Dos Palillos

Set next to Casa Camper hotel (T 93 342 6280), the Michelin-starred Dos Palillos encapsulates two gastro trends in the city: Asian cuisine and creative ways with tapas (*palillo* means both chopstick and toothpick). Chef Albert Raurich and his Japanese wife, Tamae Imachi, both former members of the elBulli team, have achieved a happy marriage of East and West in their tiny restaurant. The front bar pays homage to traditional tapas haunts of old, with strip lighting, terrazzo flooring and kitsch paraphernalia; beyond it is a darkly lit dining room (above) that may be space-challenged, but it works as an intimate setting for the intricate food. *Carrer d'Elisabets 9, T 93 304 0513, www.dospalillos.com*

Norte

For such a tiny space (just a mere six tables), Norte is hard to miss: it sits on one of Eixample's chamfered corners, visible from all directions in its dazzling luminosity. Tables, chairs and walls are all white, and the restaurant's name is written in bare bulbs above the (white) bar. For all that, it is warm and welcoming, and the cooking is all colour. The brainchild of Fernando Martínez-Conde, Lara Zaballa and María González, who met while working in the kitchens at Roca Moo (see p016), Norte brings together meticulously sourced local products, served simply. The menu is short and not prone to frequent changes, but few tire of the croquetas made with veal shank, or the chocolate mousse with peanuts and crumble.
Carrer de la Diputació 321, T 93 528 7676, www.norterestaurante.com

Big Fish
Inspired by the loft-style restaurants
of New York's Meatpacking District,
Big Fish features leather chesterfields,
mismatched tables and chairs, and 1970s
chandeliers. Mediterranean fish dishes,
such as wild sea bass, are matched with
exceptional wines, and there's a non-
stop sushi bar, with takeaway available.
*Carrer Comercial 9, T 93 268 1728,
www.bigfish.cat*

Quimet & Quimet

This pint-sized *taberna* has a faithful
following of customers from all over the
world, and many food critics cite it as a
must-do Barna experience. For nearly 100
years, Quimet & Quimet has specialised
in serving farmhouse cheeses, charcuterie
and *conservas* – seafood in a tin, often
regarded more highly in Spain than the
fresh variety. Co-owner Joaquím Peréz
arranges these ingredients with an artist's
eye, either into bite-sized *montaditos*
(various toppings on small slices of bread)
or tapas-type plates; try the cod with
black-olive tapenade or crème fraîche
with truffle-infused honey. Arrive just
before the lunchtime rush for a selection
of snacks, or at about 7pm for pre-dinner
tapas, accompanied by a glass or two
from the excellent wine list.
Carrer del Poeta Cabanyes 25, T 93 442 3142

Café Kafka

Down a sleepy side street in the Born, Café Kafka is inconspicuous from the outside, but push open the door and you could be in downtown Manhattan. Its bright, high-ceilinged dining room, just on the chic side of bohemian, is a design triumph. Owner Karel Schröder's eclectic approach brings together fleamarket finds, such as tarnished sunburst mirrors, with a showpiece sputnik light and Diesel with Foscarini lamps. Retro chairs have been upholstered in autumnal shades of velvet, and a bar with suspended vintage lights runs down one side. There is a focus on healthy eating (you can choose to have your tortilla 'low protein' or 'carb-free', for example), but a thick and tender sirloin and some sinful desserts are also offered. *Carrer de la Fusina 7, T 93 315 1776, www.cafekafka.es*

Koy Shunka

Hideki Matsuhisa's haute Mediterranean/ Asian fusion space has proved to be one of the city's most successful restaurant launches of the past few years. Interior designer Pedro Cortacans made a focal point of the Japanese *kappo*-style open kitchen, and a spot at the large, U-shaped bar is the ultimate mise en place if you're dining alone or *à deux*. A further 30 or so seats are spread across the dining room.

Koy Shunka's inventive dishes are Spanish, Japanese or a skilful mix of the two, such as the Wagyu beef with Catalan *múrgulas* (morels) or tempura scallops. No wonder many of the finest Spanish chefs, like Ferran Adrià – a fan of the restaurant since its early days – can be found at the bar while Matsuhisa orders for them. *Carrer de Copons 7, T 93 412 7939, www.koyshunka.com*

Monvínic

Described as a 'cultural centre for wine', the sleek Monvínic is a multitasking venue. In the front, the interactive wine lists enable customers to take their pick from between 3,000 and 4,000 labels, searching by origin, year or grape. At the rear, guests can dine on sophisticated Mediterranean market cuisine at the communal Corian tables. Monvínic hosts wine tastings and has a members' club, and there's a browsable research library of books on viniculture. The polished interior is the work of local designer Alfons Tost, who has combined oak floors and a brass-coloured ceiling with some imaginative lighting. Tost also designed Fastvínic (T 93 487 3241), Monvínic's relaxed café, located just next door.
Carrer de la Diputació 249, T 93 272 6187, www.monvinic.com

Pez Vela

Another hit from Grupo Tragaluz's stable of restaurants and hotels (see p028), Pez Vela dropped anchor in 2011 down at the southern tip of Platja de Sant Sebastià. It has two spaces: an industrial-chic interior of exposed pipes, white steel panels and lacquered corrugated iron, where a slick bar specialises in bespoke cocktails; and a breezy relaxed seaside terrace (above), where one might retreat for lunch after spending a morning on the beach. At any time, the simple menu offers a decent range of paellas, tapas and chargrilled meat or fish. Book in advance to secure an outdoor table, where, at night, you'll be rubbing shoulders with a mix of savvy locals and party people staying at the nearby W hotel (see p013 and p030).
Passeig Mare Nostrum 19-21,
T 93 221 6317, www.grupotragaluz.com

INSIDER'S GUIDE

CRISTIAN ZUZUNAGA, DESIGNER

Broad in scope, Cristian Zuzunaga's work spans print, sculpture, photography, textile and furniture design. Collaborations with top brands such as the Tate museums, Ligne Roset, Kvadrat and Fabergé have led the half-Catalan, half-Peruvian designer to live all over the world, but he calls Poblenou his home. 'It's creative and edgy,' he says. 'The beach is nearby and the area isn't filled with tourists.'

A passion for good design pervades Zuzunaga's leisure time; he shops at The Outpost (Carrer Rosselló 281, T 93 457 7137) for its carefully curated menswear, hats and shoes, and its creative window displays. He refuels at Mosquito (Carrer dels Carders 46, T 93 268 7569), often with pho and the 'delicious dumplings', or in summer he may head to the terrace at fish restaurant Els Pescadors (Plaça de Prim 1, T 93 225 2018). Evenings sometimes start at the Ohla's rooftop bar (see p024) where 'the view is unbeatable'; later, Boadas (Carrer dels Tallers 1, T 93 318 9592) is the perfect stop for a gin and tonic. Following this he'd recommend Moog (Carrer de l'arc del Teatre 3, T 93 301 4991), or Sala Apolo (Carrer Nou de la Rambla 113, T 93 441 4001), a splendid dance hall that has resisted modernisation despite its uber-hip clientele. These days, though, Zuzunaga tends to linger in the Parc de la Ciutadella, enjoying the 'surreal' spectacle of awestruck tourists and nonchalant old ladies. 'I love it for the clash of people from different walks of life,' he says. *For full addresses, see Resources.*

ARCHITOUR
A GUIDE TO BARCELONA'S ICONIC BUILDINGS

Barcelona has been engaged in a long love affair with architecture, but the difference between the present day and a century ago is that the city's affections were then focused on one man: Antoni Gaudí. These days it is far more profligate. A single regeneration project at Diagonal Mar (www.diagonalmar.com) attracted Jean Nouvel, EMBT, Dominique Perrault, MVRDV, Josep Lluís Mateo and Herzog & de Meuron. More recently, Enric Ruiz-Geli's sci-fi Media-TIC (Carrer de Roc Boronat 116-126) landed in the business zone in 2010, and Enric Massip-Bosch's 110m-high Torre Diagonal ZeroZero (Avinguda Diagonal 1) arrived in 2011.

Many large-scale projects in Spain have been halted due to the economic crisis, but architecture fans can take heart from smaller builds like the Biblioteca Sant Antoni (Carrer del Comte Borrell 44-46, T 93 329 7216) by local architects RCR, as well as BOPBAA's overhaul of the iconic theatre El Molino (Carrer de Vilà i Vilà 99, T 93 205 5111). Barcelona is proof that ambitious buildings such as Mercat de Santa Caterina (see p009), Torre Agbar (see p012) and the Edifici Fòrum (Parc del Fòrum, Rambla Prim 2-4) can lead the way towards urban reinvention. Whether any of the postponed structures get the green light in the current climate remains to be seen, but given the city's belief in the transformative power of architecture, there is good reason to be hopeful.

For full addresses, see Resources.

Can Framis

The redevelopment of the working-class *barri* of Poblenou has, until recently, been noteworthy for towering, private-use skyscrapers such as Torre Agbar (see p012) and ME Barcelona (see p016), many of them built on land claimed at the expense of the area's heritage of 18th- and 19th-century industrial architecture. Can Framis, an award-winning gallery for contemporary Catalan art, has changed this. The remarkable conversion of an 18th-century wool factory is the work of local architects BAAS and was completed in 2009. A stark, reinforced-concrete annexe was installed alongside a pair of existing warehouses, creating a courtyard between the three buildings (used for the gallery's lively cultural programme). *Carrer de Roc Boronat 116-126, T 93 320 8736, www.fundaciovilacasas.com*

Walden 7

Situated on the city's periphery, Walden 7 is an early work by local architect Ricardo Bofill – creator of the W hotel (see p013) – and for many it is also his greatest. Completed in 1974, the russet-coloured building looms like a modernist fortress. Inside, the modular apartments are linked by a web of elevated walkways and bridges.
Carretera Reial 106, www.walden7.com

Disseny Hub

When the delay-ridden Disseny Hub finally opens to the public in spring 2014, it will include the Design Museum (Museu del Disseny), which will merge collections of Spanish clothing and textiles, graphic arts, decorative arts, and ceramics. The zinc- and glass-clad building – already dubbed *la grapadora* (the stapler), for the way it dramatically looms over Plaça de les Glòries – was the creation of local architects MBM. Two floors are 14.5m below ground, illuminated with natural light via a clever trench system that also features a lake. Set to be just as thrilling inside, Disseny's long, low spaces will be lit by rods of kaleidoscopic LED colour running along the ceilings. Until it opens, the public can stroll around the grounds. *Plaça de les Glòries Catalanes 37-38, T 93 309 1540, www.dhub-bcn.cat*

Edifici Gas Natural

As with the Mercat de Santa Caterina (see p009), architect Benedetta Tagliabue saw through the completion of the Edifici Gas Natural, the headquarters of the Spanish gas supplier, after the untimely death of her husband and working partner Enric Miralles. Standing tall at the crossroads between Barceloneta, the old maritime district, and the modern Vila Olímpica, this brave 2008 building is the sum of its parts – an 85m-high tower, a 40m-long annexe (nicknamed the 'aircraft carrier') cantilevering off the side, and a five-storey axis in-between (we suggest viewing the work from all sides in order to appreciate its geometry). Its curtain-glass facade acts as a mirror for the surrounding skyscrapers, among which is the Hotel Arts (see p016).
Plaça del Gas 1

Pavelló Mies van der Rohe

This iconic monument to rationalism, built as the German Pavilion for the 1929 Barcelona World's Fair, is seen as a milestone in modern European architecture. All marble, onyx, steel and glass, it is the proper home for Mies van der Rohe's 'Barcelona' chair. The pavilion was disassembled in 1930, but in 1980, Oriol Bohigas, then head of urban planning at the city council, began to appoint a team to research, design and oversee its reconstruction. Ignasi de Solà-Morales, Cristian Cirici and Fernando Ramos were the selected architects. Work began in 1983 and the new building was opened on its original site in 1986. Open 10am to 8pm daily; guided tours are available on Saturdays. *Avinguda Francesc Ferrer i Guàrdia 7, T 93 423 4016, www.miesbcn.com*

SHOPPING
THE BEST RETAIL THERAPY AND WHAT TO BUY

A trip to any cultural or culinary hotspot in Barcelona should always be combined with some targeted retail therapy, as there are specialist boutiques in all the main districts. Born is best for fashion; head to the warren of streets off Passeig del Born, home to Como Agua de Mayo (Carrer de l'Argenteria 43, T 93 310 6441), which offers womenswear alongside shoes by Chie Mihara, and Le Swing (Carrer del Rec 16, T 93 310 1449), a vintage emporium. La Comercial has three individual spaces selling women's and men's clothing on Carrer del Rec (Nos 52, 73 and 75), whereas Beatriz Furest (Carrer de l'Esparteria 1, T 93 268 3796) and Iriarte Iriarte (opposite) stock handmade leather bags. Uptown, Cristina Castañer (Carrer del Mestre Nicolau 23, T 93 414 2428) has been making espadrilles for many years, and Santa Eulália (Passeig de Gràcia 93, T 93 215 0674) displays top-flight designers.

Catalan delicacies can be bought in the basement of El Corte Inglés (Plaça de Catalunya 14, T 93 306 3800), adjacent to the supermarket, and wine buffs should visit Vila Viniteca (Carrer dels Agullers 7, T 90 232 7777) for Spanish labels. La Central del Raval (Carrer d'Elisabets 6, T 90 288 4990) is one of the city's best bookshops; for specialised art and design tomes, visit La Central at MACBA (see p032) or the great *llibreria* at COAC (Plaça Nova 5, T 93 301 5000), Catalonia's architecture school.
For full addresses, see Resources.

Iriarte Iriarte

From a small workshop in Barcelona's tiny artisan zone near Museu Picasso (see p032), Carolina Iriarte produces her line of sturdy, school-inspired leather handbags, wallets and satchels, including the Mistral (above), €280. Originally from Argentina, Iriarte completes all of her accessories by hand, from the tanning process to the very last stitch, and any buckles or rivets that she doesn't make, she recycles from local suppliers. Ready-made bags are available, but most of the items here are produced to order; expect to wait up to five weeks for your bespoke creation. The workshop is open in the afternoons, or visit Iriarte's appointment-only studio/showroom at Plaça Reial 8, which opened in 2013 and displays her new collections.
Carrer Cotoners 12, T 93 319 8175, www.iriarteiriarte.com

Les Topettes

Owned by two young Spaniards who have combined their passion for design with a love of all things fragrant, Les Topettes is a bright perfumery stocking products from across the globe. Despite the small space, owners Lucía Laurin and Oriol Montañés have created a stylish modern interior, featuring glazed white bricks, vintage lamps and Macael marble flooring. It's a joy to browse and ideal if you are in need of an elegant gift to take home. Choose from beautifully packaged goat's milk soap by Portuguese brand Castelbel, or scent from Madrid-based perfume house Oliver & Co. Men are well catered for with smart toiletries by Musgo Real, and for the eco-conscious there are organic candles from Spanish brand Olivia.

Carrer de Joaquín Costa 33, T 93 500 5564, www.lestopettes.com

Oriol Balaguer

Known locally as the Christian Lacroix of cake and chocolate-making, Oriol Balaguer has won numerous awards, yet remains an aloof, serious figure within the tight-knit world of Spanish haute cuisine. Balaguer has shops in Madrid and Riyadh, but his first was this bijou corner establishment in well-heeled Barrio Alto. Inside, chocolates, mousses, cakes and pastries of the most intricate shapes, flavours and layered textures are displayed with the sort of reverence normally reserved for precious jewels, thanks to dark backdrops, spotlighting and even dry-ice effects. Purchase a tray of sweetmeats and sweet treats and a bottle of cava, then retire to the nearby Parc Turó for an indulgent picnic.
Plaça de Sant Gregori Taumaturg 2, T 93 201 1846, www.oriolbalaguer.com

Vinçon

Barcelona's leading design emporium since the 1940s, Vinçon spans two floors and has its own exhibition space, a roof terrace for garden furnishings – with views of Casa Milà (see p014) next door – and an apartment for showcasing furniture. The window displays are always a crowd-stopper, and, inside, a huge collection of home- and officewares are presented without ceremony; the humble and the high-end are casually mixed with carefree panache. Make sure that you check out Sala Vinçon, a gallery established here in 1973, focusing on graphic and industrial design. The store is the place to discover statement pieces, but for all its fame and cachet, it also stocks practical items that you'll struggle to find anywhere else. *Passeig de Gràcia 96, T 93 215 6050, www.vincon.com*

Colmado Quilez

Once upon a time, old-school grocery stores (*colmados*) were commonplace in Barcelona, but now only a handful remain. Possibly the best-loved is Colmado Quilez, which dates back to 1908. Its handsome shopfront is 40m long, and displays an incredible variety of local and international foodstuffs, from a range that is said to cover more than 10,000 products. These run from the best Catalan cheeses and charcuterie to €300 tins of caviar. You can buy the store's own-brand foie gras, get some coffee freshly ground or just a carton of milk. The most impressive section, however, is the liquids – from the 200 brands of mineral water to one of Europe's biggest selection of whiskies. There are five other branches in town. *Rambla Catalunya 63, T 93 215 2356, www.lafuente.es*

Tresserra Collection
This exquisite retro-futurist furniture
collection, designed by Jaime Tresserra,
has featured in several Almodóvar films.
The museum-worthy chairs, desks,
cabinets and tables are hand-crafted
using wood, glass, leather and nickel-
plated, hand-forged joinery. Orders
take from eight to ten weeks to finish.
Carrer de Josep Bertrand 17,
T 93 200 4922, www.tresserra.com

Mutt

Part gallery, part bookshop, Mutt fills a much-needed gap in the city for a venue that is prepared to take risks. Situated in a large, late 19th-century building, its high white walls accommodate temporary shows from bleeding-edge creatives, such as artists Blanca Miró Skoudy, Rubenimichi, Sosaku Miyazaki, Pau Sampera and Miju Lee. Mutt's wide selection of magazines and books on art, counterculture and graphic design will delight; check out titles from local publisher Alpha Decay, whose retro-inspired illustrated covers make them highly collectable, or the range of books on Barcelona, covering everything from its heritage to its urban legends. *Carrer del Comerç 15, T 93 192 4438, www.mutt.es*

Loewe

Luxury Spanish brand Loewe has its Barcelona flagship in what was already a spectacular space within modernista architect Lluís Domènech i Montaner's Casa Lleó Morera. A fantastical stuccoed building, it was renovated in 2012. New York-based architect Peter Marino was in charge of the interior design, which now features a vertical garden and floors paved with Tanzanian and Madagascan stone; some original elements are still visible, especially in the frescoed ceilings. Luggage, fashion and accessories are spread over three floors. Further along Passeig de Gràcia is the Galería Loewe (overleaf; T 93 200 0920), which opened in 2012 and has some of the brand's most iconic pieces on show.
Passeig de Gràcia 35, T 93 216 0400, www.loewe.com

SPORTS AND SPAS
WORK OUT, CHILL OUT OR JUST WATCH

Football is Spain's most cherished sport by far, and Barcelona is particularly enamoured of the beautiful game due to its two La Liga teams. The famed home of FC Barcelona, Camp Nou (Carrer d'Aristides Maillol, T 90 218 9900), includes a museum, and there are tours of the stadium, which has a capacity of 98,787. Tickets to actual games are harder to come by; you'll have more luck finding seats to watch the less-famous RCD Espanyol, who moved in 2009 to a new stadium, Estadi RCDE (Avinguda del Baix Llobregat 100, T 90 290 3912). Thanks to the legacy of the 1992 Olympics, the city hosts numerous events every year, the most renowned of which is the F1 Spanish Grand Prix at the Circuit de Catalunya (Montmeló, T 93 571 9700), when almost every hotel in town is fully booked.

Barcelona's beaches get packed in summer, but are perfect for a morning jog or a stroll before the sun-worshippers descend. Start at Barceloneta and follow the boardwalk to Hotel Arts (see p016) and Port Olímpic. If the heat is stifling, head for Carretera de les Aigües in Tibidabo for mountain air and some great panoramas. Thanks to new lanes across the city, cycling has really taken off. Bicycles can be hired at Un Cotxe Menys (Carrer Esparteria 3, T 93 268 2105) or from most tourist offices, where they come with a map of routes. Otherwise, Bike Rental Barcelona (T 66 605 7655, www.bikerentalbarcelona.com) can deliver a model to your hotel.

For full addresses, see Resources.

The Spa by Six Senses

Located on the 42nd and 43rd floors of Hotel Arts (see p016), this sun-filled spa is not to be missed for its stunning views of the Med. A selection of two-and-a-half-hour packages are on offer, and rooms are equipped with chromotherapy features to adapt their colour and mood. Treatments are generally faithful to Six Senses' Asian values – Thai massages and Indian head massages are available – but there's also a subtle nod to the locale, found in offerings such as the Hot Stone Chocolate Massage, €245, which utilises Catalan chocolate oil. Facilities include separate wet areas for men and women, saunas, steam rooms, and a relaxation area that has outdoor terraces (above). Book well ahead as the hotel guests have priority here.
Carrer de la Marina 19-21, T 93 224 7067, www.sixsenses.com

Anella Olímpica

It's no secret that the 1992 Olympics turned Barcelona's fortunes round, but a lesser-known part of the Games' legacy is the Anella Olímpica, a collection of sports facilities in Montjuïc created by leading architects. The main stadium, the Estadi Olímpic, was in fact designed for the 1929 World's Fair, but was fully renovated for the Olympics by Federico Correa, Alfonso Milá and others; until 2009 it was RCD Espanyol's home ground. The high-tech indoor arena, Palau Sant Jordi (above), was designed by Japanese architect Arata Isozaki, and in 2014 it will co-host the FIBA Basketball World Cup. Nearby is the Museu Olímpic i de l'Esport (T 93 292 5379), and towering over it all, like a white needle piercing the skyline, is Santiago Calatrava's communications tower.
Parc de Montjuïc, T 93 426 2089

Mandarin Oriental Spa

Set in the Mandarin Oriental (see p022), on Barcelona's most elegant boulevard, this is a wonderfully chic facility in a city where spa culture generally extends to ladies who lunch and deep-pocketed tourists. Charcoal slate walls and the gentle chink of *tingshas* (Tibetan cymbals) make this a calming experience; try not to drift off in the relaxation room (above) before your treatment. The menu runs from the 25-minute Anti Jet Lag massage, to the full-day Detox for Wellness, which involves an algae body wrap, a massage and a facial. Hotel guests have access to a rooftop pool, open in summer; otherwise the 12m heated indoor pool (opposite) is a good alternative for day visitors, or those too chilled to make the schlep upstairs. *Passeig de Gràcia 38-40, T 93 151 8888, www.mandarinoriental.com/barcelona*

Zona de Banys

The 2004 Universal Forum of Cultures was widely criticised for its cost and 'necessity', but its infrastructure has proved to be considerably more sustainable than the event itself. Along with the wide, sloping squares and promenades on the site, and Herzog & de Meuron's Edifici Fòrum (see p064), Zona de Banys' appeal has endured. The work of local architect Beth Galí, who has produced a quiet storm in urban spaces (she also remodelled Barcelona's acclaimed Parc de Joan Miró and designed the Fossar de la Pedrera monument), Zona de Banys is the most secluded and visually appealing place to swim along the city's shores. A long wooden boardwalk hugs the coastline and provides somewhere to catch the sun. The concrete platforms can be used for diving and they also break the waves, ensuring a safe and serene dip.
Parc del Fòrum, Rambla de Prim 1

ESCAPES

WHERE TO GO IF YOU WANT TO LEAVE TOWN

Although Barcelona's beaches and Montjuïc park provide respite from the urban hustle, a day in the country or on the Costa Brava offers a superior breather. A trip to the Teatre-Museu Dalí (Plaça Gala-Salvador Dalí 5, T 97 267 7500) in Figueres can be combined with a visit to the artist's home in Cadaqués (Portlligat, T 97 225 1015; booking essential). Montserrat's jagged cliffs and monastery are a must for nature lovers and rock climbers; Catalonia's wine country, the Penedès, is just beyond. Take the train to the town of Vilafranca to tour the fin-de-siècle bodegas of cava producer Codorníu (Avinguda Jaume Codorníu, Sant Sadurní d'Anoia, T 93 891 3342), and book into Can Bonastre (Carretera B-224 km13.2, Masquefa, T 93 772 8767), a luxury resort ringed by vineyards.

For some sea air, head south-west to Sitges (opposite) or north-east to Sant Pol de Mar, home of the celebrated Restaurant Sant Pau (Carrer Nou 10, T 93 760 0662; closed Sunday, Monday and Thursday lunchtimes). An hour north-east by train is Girona (see p098); the city's surrounding countryside is dotted with lovely villages and little-known gems, including hotel Mas de Torrent (Afores de Torrent, T 90 255 0321). In winter, the Vall de Núria offers gentle skiing, and further north, the Pyrenean town of Puigcerdà is a cosy base for ski resorts, particularly the luxury Villa Paulita (Avinguda Pons i Gasch 15, T 97 288 4622).

For full addresses, see Resources.

Sitges

This resort, beloved by Barcelonins and gay visitors of all nationalities, is only a 40-minute scenic train journey from Passeig de Gràcia or Sants train stations. Leave early to guarantee a decent space on the sand: just north of the port, the Platja de Balmins is a good, quiet spot. Be aware that primarily it's a nudist beach, but not exclusively so. After a morning soaking up the sun, head for a light lunch at the sea-facing Tambucho (T 93 894 7912), then spend the afternoon meandering through the town's winding streets. Stop off at the Museu Romàntic (T 93 894 2969), a late 18th-century mansion that shows what domestic life was like in Sitges' golden age. Finish the day with dinner at Alfresco (T 93 894 0600; Thursday to Saturday) before catching the last train back to Barcelona.

El Celler de Can Roca, Girona

Girona is Barcelona in miniature, minus the multiculturalism and the tourists. Its medieval quarter is one of the best preserved Jewish ghettoes in Europe. Before arriving, book a table at El Celler de Can Roca, the Roca brothers' modish three-Michelin-starred restaurant (voted the world's best in 2013) in an annexe attached to a stone *masia* (farmhouse). *Can Sunyer 48, T 97 222 2157*

Ferrer Bobet, Tarragona

As a wine-growing zone, the Priorat is well established locally, and widely recognised internationally as one of the country's best. It's taken rather longer for the needs of the visiting wine-lover to be met, but a spate of recent openings, in the form of sleek destination wineries to rival those of La Rioja, is set to change all that. The first to open its doors was Ferrer Bobet, designed by Barcelona-based architects Espinet/Ubach. Their structure of stone, concrete, wood and glass hovers high above the steep slate-soil terraces that have made the region and its beefy reds so famous. Ferrer Bobet's youthful viniculturists are also making waves with their new-style wines made from 100-year-old *Garnatxa* (Grenache) vines. *Carretera Falset a Porrera (T-740), T 60 994 5532, www.ferrerbobet.com*

Consolación, Matarraña

A three-hour drive from Barcelona, in the pine-clad hills of the Matarraña on the borders of Catalonia and Aragón, is the Consolación hotel. A sympathetically restored 16th-century hermitage forms the backbone of a building containing modern bedrooms, an accomplished restaurant and a library. Distributed around the grounds, however, are the main attraction: the Kubes (pictured).

These are guest rooms in the guise of gravity-defying, glass-fronted boxes tacked on to the hillside, with views over the treetops. The monochrome interiors are minimal yet supremely comfortable, and each Kube has a sunken slate bath to facilitate the ultimate recovery after exploring the surrounding landscape. *Monroyo, Teruel, T 97 885 6755, www.consolacion.com.es*

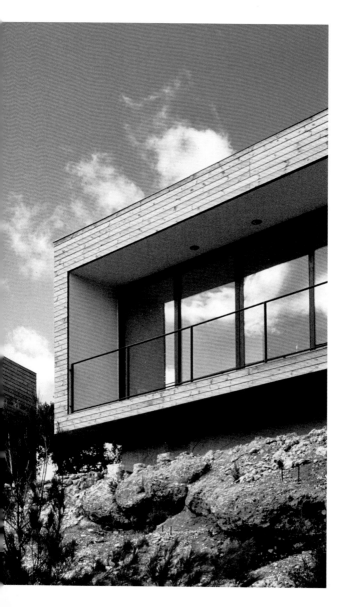

NOTES
SKETCHES AND MEMOS

RESOURCES

CITY GUIDE DIRECTORY

A

Alfresco 097
 Carrer Pau Barrabeitg 4
 Sitges
 T 93 894 0600
 www.alfrescorestaurante.es
Anella Olímpica 090
 Parc de Montjuïc
 T 93 426 2089
Las Arenas 009
 Gran Via de les Corts Catalanes 373-385
 T 93 289 0244
 www.arenasdebarcelona.com

B

Beatriz Furest 072
 Carrer de l'Espartería 1
 T 93 268 3796
 www.beatrizfurest.com
Biblioteca Sant Antoni 064
 Carrer del Comte Borrell 44-46
 T 93 329 7216
Big Fish 054
 Carrer Comercial 9
 T 93 268 1728
 www.bigfish.cat
Bike Rental Barcelona 088
 T 66 605 7655
 www.bikerentalbarcelona.com
Bliss Spa 030
 W hotel
 Plaça de la Rosa dels Vents 1
 T 93 295 2658
 www.w-barcelona.com
Boadas 062
 Carrer dels Tallers 1
 T 93 318 9592
 www.boadascocktails.com

Boca Grande 050
 Passatge de la Concepció 12
 T 93 467 5149
 www.bocagrande.cat
Bravo 030
 W hotel
 Plaça de la Rosa dels Vents 1
 T 93 295 2636
 www.w-barcelona.com

C

Café Kafka 057
 Carrer de la Fusina 7
 T 93 315 1776
 www.cafekafka.es
CaixaForum 032
 Avinguda de Francesc Ferrer
 i Guàrdia 6-8
 T 93 476 8600
 www.fundacio.lacaixa.es
Camp Nou 088
 Carrer d'Arístides Maillol
 T 90 218 9900
 www.fcbarcelona.com
Can Framis 065
 Carrer de Roc Boronat 116-126
 T 93 320 8736
 www.fundaciovilacasas.com
Can Ravell 040
 Carrer d'Aragó 313
 T 93 457 5114
 www.ravell.com
Casa Amatller 034
 Passeig de Gràcia 41
 www.amatller.org

HOTELS

ADDRESSES AND ROOM RATES

Alma 017
Room rates:
double, from €175
Carrer de Mallorca 271
T 93 216 4490
www.almabarcelona.com

Hotel Arts 016
Room rates:
double, from €295
Carrer de la Marina 19–21
T 93 221 1000
www.hotelartsbarcelona.com

Axel Hotel 016
Room rates:
double, from €120
Carrer d'Aribau 33
T 93 323 9393
www.axelhotels.com

Bagués Hotel 020
Room rates:
double, from €160;
Jewel Suite, from €370
La Rambla 105
T 93 343 5000
www.derbyhotels.com

Barceló Raval 029
Room rates:
double, from €110;
Junior Suite, €190
Rambla del Raval 17–21
T 93 320 1490
www.barcelo.com

Can Bonastre 096
Room rates:
double, from €280
Carretera B-224 km13.2
Masquefa
T 93 772 8767
www.canbonastre.com

Claris Hotel 016
Room rates:
double, €135
Carrer de Pau Claris 150
T 93 487 6262
www.derbyhotels.com

Consolación 102
Room rates:
double, €145;
Kube, from €170
Monroyo
Matarraña
Teruel
T 97 885 6755
www.consolacion.com.es

Hotel Do: Plaça Reial 023
Room rates:
double, €260;
Junior Suite, from €490
Plaça Reial 1
T 93 481 3666
www.hoteldoreial.com

Hotel 1898 016
Room rates:
double, from €230
La Rambla 109
T 93 552 9552
www.hotel1898.com

Hotel España 016
Room rates:
double, from €150
Carrer de Sant Pau 9-11
T 93 550 0000
www.hotelespanya.com

Mandarin Oriental 022
  Room rates:
  double, from €395;
  Barcelona Suite, from €4,720
  Passeig de Gràcia 38-40
  T 93 151 8888
  www.mandarinoriental.com/barcelona

Mas de Torrent 096
  Room rates:
  suite, from €300
  Afores de Torrent
  Girona
  T 90 255 0321
  www.mastorrent.com

ME 016
  Room rates:
  double, from €135
  Carrer de Pere IV 272
  T 93 367 2050
  www.me-barcelona.com

Mercer Hotel 018
  Room rates:
  double, from €270;
  Gran Deluxe, €320
  Carrer dels Lledó 7
  T 93 310 2387
  www.mercerbarcelona.com

The Mirror 016
  Room rates:
  double, from €105
  Carrer de Còrsega 255
  T 93 202 8686
  www.themirrorbarcelona.com

Ohla Hotel 024
  Room rates:
  double, from €200;
  Junior Suite, from €300
  Vìa Laietana 49
  T 93 341 5050
  www.ohlahotel.com

Hotel Omm 028
  Room rates:
  double, from €210;
  Omm King, €625;
  Superior Room, €730
  Carrer Rosselló 265
  T 93 445 4000
  www.hotelomm.es

El Palauet 026
  Suite, from €500;
  Principal Tibidabo Suite, from €700
  Passeig de Gràcia 113
  T 93 218 0050
  www.eplivingbarcelona.com

Suites Avenue 031
  Room rates:
  apartment, from €220;
  Pedrera Penthouse, from €415
  Passeig de Gràcia 83
  T 93 487 4159
  www.derbyhotels.com

Villa Paulita 096
  Room rates:
  double, from €120
  Avinguda Pons i Gasch 15
  Puigcerdà
  T 97 288 4622
  www.villapaulitahotel.com

W 030
  Room rates:
  double, from €300;
  Cool Corner Suite, from €1,815
  Plaça de la Rosa dels Vents 1
  T 93 295 2800
  www.w-barcelona.com

WALLPAPER* CITY GUIDES

Executive Editor
Rachael Moloney

Editor
Ella Marshall
Authors
Sally Davies
Suzanne Wales

Art Director
Loran Stosskopf
Art Editor
Eriko Shimazaki
Designer
Mayumi Hashimoto
Map Illustrator
Russell Bell

Photography Editor
Elisa Merlo
Assistant Photography Editor
Nabil Butt

Chief Sub-Editor
Nick Mee
Sub-Editor
Farah Shafiq

Editorial Assistant
Emma Harrison

Interns
Phil James
Rodrigo Marquez
Jana Otte
Maja Šćepanović

Wallpaper* Group Editor-in-Chief
Tony Chambers
Publishing Director
Gord Ray
Managing Editor
Oliver Adamson

Contributors
Jeroen Bergmans
Marta Puigdemasa
Tara Stevens

Wallpaper* ® is a
registered trademark
of IPC Media Limited

First published 2006
Revised and updated
2008, 2009, 2010,
2011 and 2013

All prices are correct at
the time of going to press,
but are subject to change.

Printed in China

PHAIDON

Phaidon Press Limited
Regent's Wharf
All Saints Street
London N1 9PA

Phaidon Press Inc
180 Varick Street
New York, NY 10014

Phaidon® is a registered
trademark of Phaidon
Press Limited

www.phaidon.com

A CIP Catalogue record for
this book is available from
the British Library.

ISBN 978 0 7148 6631 4

PHOTOGRAPHERS

Palmer Aldritch
Hotel Omm, p028
The Spa by Six
Senses, p089

Iñigo Bujedo Aguirre
Disseny Hub, p068

Lluís Casals
Ferrer Bobet, pp100-101

Roger Casas
Barcelona city view,
inside front cover
Torre Agbar, p012
W hotel, p013
Casa Milà, pp014-015
Alma, p017
Mercer Hotel, p018, p019
Bagués Hotel, pp020-021
Hotel DO: Plaça Reial, p023
Ohla Hotel, p024, p025
El Palauet, pp026-027
Barceló Raval, p029
Suites Avenue, p031
Cornelia and Co, p033
Casa Batlló, p034
CCCB, p035
Fundació Joan
Miró, pp036-037
41° Experience, p038
Tickets, p039

Chez Cocó, p041
MAT Bar, pp042-043
Velódromo, p044
Dry Martini, p045
Ocaña, pp046-047
Cinc Sentits, pp048-049
Boca Chica, p050,
Boca Grande, p051
Norte, p053
Big Fish, pp054-055
Quimet & Quimet, p056
Café Kafka, p057
Koy Shunka, pp058-059
Pez Vela, p061
Cristian Zuzunaga, p063
Can Framis, p065
Edifici Gas Natural, p069
Pavelló Mies van der Rohe,
pp070-071
Les Topettes, pp074-075
Oriol Balaguer, p076, p077
Vinçon, pp078-079
Colmado Quilez,
p080, p081
Tresserra Collection,
pp082-083
Mutt, p084
Loewe, p085
Galería Loewe, pp086-087
Anella Olímpica,
pp090-091
Mandarin Oriental
Spa, p092, p093
Zona de Banys, pp094-095
Sitges, p097

Peartree Digital
Iriarte Iriarte bag, p073

Pedro Pegenaute
Mandarin Oriental, p022
Walden 7, pp066-067

BARCELONA
A COLOUR-CODED GUIDE TO THE HOT 'HOODS

EIXAMPLE
The heartland of modernista architecture should be the first port of call for Gaudí fans

BARRI GÒTIC
Barna's historic core is a warren of medieval lanes encircling the flamboyant cathedral

BARCELONETA
This salty, low-rise, maritime district is bordered by a collection of brave new skyscrapers

GRÀCIA
Often ignored by tourists en route to Gaudí's Parc Güell, this is the city's emerging area

POBLE SEC
Head to the leafy squares and quiet streets of this charming district for a change of pace

POBLENOU
Home to an emerging high-rise business zone, and a new generation of loft-living locals

RAVAL
Now arguably Barcelona's cultural epicentre, Raval brims with bars and boutiques

SANT PERE/BORN
For great shopping and a sedate vision of the city as it used to be, head here. But do it fast

For a full description of each neighbourhood, see the Introduction.
Featured venues are colour-coded, according to the district in which they are located.